Learning to Write
Nouns

WEIGL PUBLISHERS INC.

Published by Weigl Publishers Inc.
350 5th Avenue, Suite 3304, PMB 6G
New York, NY 10118-0069

Website: www.weigl.com

All of the Internet URLs given in the book were valid at the time of publication. However, due to the
dynamic nature of the Internet, some addresses may have changed, or sites may have ceased to exist
since publication. While the author and publisher regret any inconvenience this may cause readers,
no responsibility for any such changes can be accepted by either the author or the publisher.

Library of Congress Cataloging-in-Publication Data

Lambert, Deborah.
 Nouns / Deborah Lambert.
    p. cm.
 Includes webliography and index.
 ISBN 978-1-60596-046-3 (hard cover : alk. paper) -- ISBN 978-1-60596-047-0 (soft cover : alk.
paper)
 1. English language--Noun--Juvenile literature. I. Title.
 PE1201.L36 2009
 428.2--dc22
                          2009001952

Printed in China
1 2 3 4 5 6 7 8 9 0 13 12 11 10 09

Editor: Deborah G. Lambert
Design: Terry Paulhus

Photograph Credits

Weigl acknowledges Getty images as its image supplier for this title.

All of the internet URLs given in the book were valid at the time of publication. However, due to the
dynamic nature of the internet, some addresses may have changed, or sites may have ceased to exist
since publication. While the author and publisher regret any inconvenience this may cause readers,
no responsibility for any such changes can be accepted by either the author or the publisher.

Every reasonable effort has been made to trace ownership and to obtain permission to reprint
copyright material. The publishers would be pleased to have any errors or omissions brought
to their attention so that they may be corrected in subsequent printings.

Table of Contents

4   What is a Noun?

6   Identifying Types of Nouns

8   Learning about Proper Nouns

10   Learning about Common Nouns

12   Learning about Possessive Nouns

14   Where Do They Belong?

16   Using Nouns to Create Sentences

18   Tools for Learning about Nouns

20   Put Your Knowledge to Use

22   Other Parts of Speech

23   Further Research

24   Glossary/Index

What is a Noun?

A noun is a part of speech that is usually used to name a person, place, or thing. The words shaded red in this paragraph about family life in the Polynesian **culture** are all nouns.

Polynesians *often had large* families *with many* children. *Aunts, uncles, grandparents,* and *cousins had very close* relationships. *When* family members *would travel to another* island, *the remaining* family *became worried. To make sure that they were safe, the remaining family would pass a piece of coconut* skin *under the travelers'* canoe *before it set sail. The coconut skin was then placed under a* rock. *It was removed only when the worried family members felt their traveling* relatives *should have arrived safely.*

In the paragraph, examples of persons include "Polynesians," "families," "children," and "uncles." An example of a place is "island." "Skin" and "rock" are examples of things.

In your notebook, write down the other nouns from the paragraph, and show whether they refer to persons, places, or things.

To read more about Polynesian culture, go to **www.pakahiki. com/polynesia/culture-of-polynesia**, and look for more examples of nouns.

Finding the Nouns

The following paragraphs tell a story about family life in Aboriginal Australian culture. They describe how boys and girls are **initiated** into their culture. They also talk about the respect given to elders and the role of healers.

Look for all the nouns in this paragraph. Then, place them in a table like the one on this page. Three examples have been done for you.

Young Aboriginal Australians learn sacred stories during initiation ceremonies and gatherings. Initiation ceremonies mark the passage of a child into adulthood. For girls, these ceremonies are usually quite simple. For boys, these ceremonies may take several years to complete. They learn the traditions and sacred stories of the group. After a boy completes his final ceremony, he can marry.

While all members of an Aboriginal group are considered equals, the elder members receive the most respect. This is because the elders have the most knowledge to share. They teach younger Aboriginal Australians how to be responsible for, and respect the land, sea, people, and the Aboriginal culture.

Person(s)	Place(s)	Thing(s)
Aboriginal Australians, elder	sea	stories

To read more about Aboriginal Australian culture, go to **http://indigenous australia.frogandtoad.com.au**. Look for more examples of nouns on this website, and place some of them in your chart.

Identifying Types of Nouns

There are many types of nouns. Some of the main types include proper, common, and possessive nouns.

Proper nouns name specific persons, places, or things and always begin with a capital letter. Common nouns refer to persons, places, or things in a general sense. Possessive nouns show ownership by adding an apostrophe and *s* to singular nouns and only an apostrophe to plural nouns.

Examples of proper, common, and possessive nouns are shaded red in this paragraph about the history of the Maori.

New Zealand's, or Aotearoa's, indigenous peoples are called the Maori. When the Maori arrived at Aotearoa, they found a land different to the tropical islands they came from. The temperature was cooler. There were different plants and trees. There were no land mammals, just reptiles, birds, and sea animals.

This chart shows which words are proper, common, and possessive nouns in the paragraph. Now, draw a chart like this one, and place the other nouns in the paragraph in their proper rows.

Types of Nouns	Examples
Proper	Maori, Aotearoa
Common	peoples, islands, trees
Possessive	New Zealand's

Visit **www.newzealandnz.co.nz/maori** to learn more about the Maori.

Selecting Types of Nouns

These paragraphs describe the way of life of **indigenous peoples** called Inuit. Read the paragraphs, and make a list of the types of nouns used. Then, next to each one, name the type of noun.

The Inuit live in the Arctic areas of Canada, Greenland, Russia, and the United States. Family has always been very important to them. Groups of hunting families live and work together to increase their chances of finding and sharing food. In Inuit society, men and women have different roles. The men fish, hunt, and build houses. The women skin the animals and dry their meat. They also cook and sew clothes.

Inuit groups move from place to place throughout the year. The group camps for a few months in places where there are many animals to hunt. Each group is much like one big family. Some people act as leaders, but they do not tell other group members what to do. Instead, they listen to people and offer advice. These leaders are often the oldest members of the group.

Visit **www.ih.k12.oh.us/ps/Inuit/Maininuit.htm** to learn more about the Inuit. Look for the different types of nouns on this website, and add them to your list.

Learning about Proper Nouns

Proper nouns are the names of specific people, places, or things. They should always begin with a capital letter. These nouns can be singular or plural.

Proper nouns that are singular name *one* specific person, place, or thing. Proper nouns that are plural name *more than one* specific person, place, or thing.

In these sentences about the Maasai, the proper nouns are shaded red. Make a list of these nouns in your notebook. Then, next to each noun, state whether it is the name of a specific person, place, or thing and if it is singular or plural.

*The **ancestors** of the Maasai originated from North Africa.*

The Maasai Girls Education Fund pays education costs for Maasai girls.

The Maasai have borrowed words from other languages, including English, Arabic, and Swahili.

Go to **www.bluegecko.org/kenya/tribes/maasai/history.htm** to learn more about the Maasai.

Identifying Proper Nouns

Mongols are the indigenous peoples of Mongolia, a country in east Asia. Read these sentences about Mongols. Make a list of all the proper nouns used. Then, place them in their correct columns in a chart like the one on this page.

Most Mongols believe in Shamanism or Lamaism.

During his rule, Genghis Khan took control of all the Mongol tribes.

By the time Kublai Khan was in power, the Mongolian Empire was at its largest. It stretched across Europe and Asia, between Hungary and Korea, and from Siberia to Tibet.

Mongols celebrate the Lunar New Year and the festival Naadam.

During the Naadam festival, men compete in the Three Games of Men, which include wrestling, **archery***, and horse racing. Children compete in the Naadam races.*

PROPER NOUNS					
Person		**Place**		**Thing**	
Singular	Plural	Singular	Plural	Singular	Plural
Genghis Khan	Mongols	Asia	Hungary and Korea	Lamaism	Three Games of Men

Visit **www.mongoliatoday.com** to learn more about Mongols today. Look for the proper nouns on this website, and add them to your list.

Learning about Common Nouns

Common nouns refer to persons, places, or things in a general sense. They do not begin with a capital letter unless they are titles of stories or at the beginning of sentences. They can be singular or plural.

Common nouns that are singular name *one* person, place, or thing. Proper nouns that are plural name *more than one* person, place, or thing.

Common nouns are used in these paragraphs about Maori art. Some of these nouns are shaded red.

Art is an important part of Maori culture. The Maori decorate the walls, pillars, and ceilings of their homes. They decorate their clothes, weapons, boats, personal objects, and even their bodies, too.

Inside the homes of Maori chiefs, the wood is carved with very detailed patterns. The Maori sometimes carve their ancestors' faces or their own faces into the wood. They also recreate the shapes of fish, whales, animals, or their gods.

In the first paragraph, "culture" is a singular common noun and is a thing. "Walls" and "homes" are plural common nouns that are things.

In your notebook, make a list of the other common nouns in the second paragraph. Then, next to each noun, state whether it is the name of a person, place, or thing and if it is singular or plural.

Identifying Common Nouns

In these paragraphs about the Mongols, some common nouns have been used. Read the paragraphs, and make a list of the common nouns. Then, draw a chart like the one on this page, and place each noun in its proper column.

The Mongols are a nomadic people. This means they travel often, moving their herds to new grazing land or to escape harsh weather. Mongols traditionally lived in family units. Each unit had a husband, one or more wives, and their children. All the families live in yurts, or felt tents.

Many unspoken rules guide Mongol life. For example, Mongols do not stare into the eyes of an elder, and a woman has to cover her mouth when she laughs. Mongols also point with all their fingers—to use just one finger is considered rude. A yurt is always open to any hungry, tired traveler, even if the owner is not at home.

COMMON NOUNS					
Persons		Places		Things	
Singular	Plural	Singular	Plural	Singular	Plural
husband	people	land	yurts	finger	herds

Learning about Possessive Nouns

Possessive nouns show ownership or belonging. Possession or belonging is shown by adding an apostrophe and "s" to the noun that owns the object. This can be done to both singular and plural nouns. Only the apostrophe is added for most plural nouns ending in the letter "s."

Some possessive nouns have been used in these sentences about the Yanomami, a group of indigenous peoples from South America. They are shaded red.

In the Yanomami culture, the burden basket rests on a *woman's* back like a backpack.

Women's duties include caring for the village children, harvesting the gardens, and cooking.

Young *warriors'* training helps them to provide for their families.

In the first sentence, "woman" is the noun, and the "back" belongs to her. An apostrophe followed by an "s" has been added to the singular noun "woman" to show the possessive form "woman's."

In the second sentence, "women's" is a possessive pronoun. An apostrophe followed by an "s" has been added to the plural noun "women" to show the possessive form "women's."

In the third sentence, "warriors" is a possessive pronoun. Only the apostrophe is added for this plural noun because it ends with an "s."

Identifying Possessive Nouns

Read these sentences about the Yanomami. Then, in your notebook, make a list of all the possessive nouns used in these sentences.

In one of the Yanomami's legends, the Moon's blood causes people to fight and kill one another.

The men's clothing include a type of apron that covers the lower half of their bodies.

The Yanomami believe that the jaguar's spirit eats dead people's souls.

Building the community's house is a job that is shared by every member of the community.

Parrots' feathers are often used to make ceremonial headgear.

Headpieces are also made from the toucan's feathers.

*All the food served during a ceremony must come from the **host**'s garden.*

All food parts are eaten by the Yanomami, including animals' skin and bones.

Games are an important part of the children's lives.

To learn more about the Yanomami, go to **http://indian-cultures.com/Cultures/yanomamo.html**. Look for the possessive nouns on this website, and add them to your list.

Where Do They Belong?

In learning to use nouns, you should be able to identify the types of nouns when they are used. In this paragraph about the type of foods the Maasai eat, many nouns have been used. Some of these nouns are shaded red.

Cattle are important to the Maasai's diet. Cow's milk makes adults and children healthy. It is also used to make yogurt and a substance similar to butter. Cows are very valuable. Therefore, the Maasai do not often kill them. They are only killed for special occasions. Maasai will not eat a cow's meat and drink its milk on the same day. When an animal is killed, everyone who has not drunk the milk will eat the meat. They believe that doing this will keep them from getting sick. The Maasai's diet also includes maize, rice, potatoes, and cabbage.

In the paragraph, examples of common nouns include "butter," "cattle," and "adults." "Butter" is a singular noun. "Cattle" and "adults" are plural nouns. "Maasai's" is an example of a possessive noun.

Make a list of the other nouns in the paragaph. What types of nouns are they?

Grouping Nouns

Select all of the nouns in these sentences about the Polynesians. Then, in your notebook, place them in a chart like the one on this page. A few examples have been done for you.

The Polynesians have created a unique culture based on their rich history, society, and beliefs.

The Polynesians live on the Pacific Islands, which include the Cook Islands, Easter Island, Hawai'i, French Polynesia, Tonga, Samoa, and Aotearoa.

The Polynesians' ancestors settled on the Pacific Islands thousands of years ago.

King Kamehameha I was a very powerful Hawai'ian ruler who helped to unite the Hawai'ian islands.

NOUNS					
Proper		**Common**		**Possessive**	
Singular	Plural	Singular	Plural	Singular	Plural
Polynesians	Cook Islands	society	beliefs	Sun's	Polynesians'

Using Nouns to Create Sentences

Imagine trying to write sentences, paragraphs, or stories without nouns. How would others know who, what, or where you are talking about? Nouns help to make sentences, for example, make sense.

In this paragraph about the Yanomami, the nouns are shaded red. Try reading the sentences aloud without the nouns. Do they make sense to you?

Make a list of all the nouns in this paragraph. Use some of these nouns to write two sentences about the cultural beliefs of the Yanomami. One has been done for you.

> The Yanomami believe that the land has a spirit.

The Yanomami believe that everything in the world has a spirit. They believe that if they care for the land and use it wisely, it will provide for them. They also believe that the fate of all people is linked to the fate of the **environment**. This ties in with the belief that, by destroying the environment, society is killing itself.

Creating Your Own Sentences Using Types of Nouns

Look at the image on this page. It shows Polynesians dancing the **hula**. There are many forms of hula dance. Each tells a unique story about Polynesian culture. Some tell the story of Earth's creation. Others tell stories about heroes and chiefs.

Try writing three sentences about what you see in the image. Use the types of nouns explained in this book. You can also use the Internet, or visit the library to find out more information about the different forms of the hula dance in the Polynesian culture. This will help you as you write your sentences.

Tools for Learning about Nouns

What did you learn? Look at the topics in the "Skills" column. Compare them to the page number in the "Page" column. Review the content you learned about nouns by reading the "Content" column below.

SKILLS	CONTENT	PAGE
Defining a noun	Polynesian culture, Aboriginal Australian culture	4–5
Identifying types of nouns	History of the Maori, Inuit culture	6–7
Learning about proper nouns	The Maasai, the Mongols	8–9
Learning about common nouns	Maori art, the Mongols	10–11
Learning about possessive nouns	Yanomami culture	12–13
Grouping nouns according to type	The Maasai diet, the Polynesians	14–15
Using nouns	Yanomami beliefs, Polynesian dance	16–17

Practice Writing Your Own Paragraphs
Using Different Types of Nouns

Face painting is used by many indigenous peoples for ceremonies or other celebrations. Go to **www.face-painting-fun.com/cultural-face-painting.html** for more information about how and why people from different cultures paint their faces.

Using the types of nouns you learned in this book, write two paragraphs describing how and why the people from two of these cultures paint their faces. Here are two pictures showing how the faces of an Aboriginal Australian boy and a Yanomami girl are being painted for one of their ceremonies.

Aboriginal Australians often paint their faces and bodies for many types of ceremonies and rituals. People of all ages, including children, take part in these ceremonies and rituals.

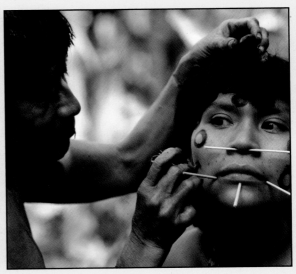

Yanomamis often paint each other for celebrations.

Put Your Knowledge to Use

Read the following paragraphs about what the Aboriginal Australians and Inuit children do for fun. There are many nouns in these paragraphs. Use as many of these nouns as you can to write two paragraphs comparing what you do for fun with that of the Aboriginal Australian and Inuit children.

For fun, the children in Aboriginal Australian culture play with dolls made of twigs and clay. They pretend to be either the mother or the father. Girls play with smaller versions of their mother's digging stick. Boys practice throwing small spears. Children also play ball games, and climb trees.

For fun, Inuit children play games, such as arm pulling, kickball, high kicks, seal-hop, and tag. They also play games, such as sky tossing, which is the first form of trampoline. To play, one person stands in the center of a large piece of dried animal hide. Many other people stand

around the hide, holding the edges. As they pull the edges, the person standing in the center of the hide is tossed into the air.

se the Internet, or visit the library to find information about a
roup of indigenous peoples of your choice. Try writing a short
ory describing what the adults do for fun. Use the types of
ouns that you learned in this book in your story.

ou can start with the following picture showing some Maasai
erforming one of their dances.

EXPANDED CHECKLIST

eread your sentences, paragraphs, or stories to make sure that you
ave all of the following.

☑ Proper nouns that are singular and plural

☑ Common nouns that are singular and plural

☑ Possessive nouns that are singular and plural

Other Parts of Speech

You have now learned the tools for using nouns. You can use your knowledge of nouns to write clear and interesting sentences, paragraphs, or stories. There are four other parts of speech. You can use some of the same tools you learned in this book to use these other parts of speech. The chart below shows the other parts of speech and their key features.

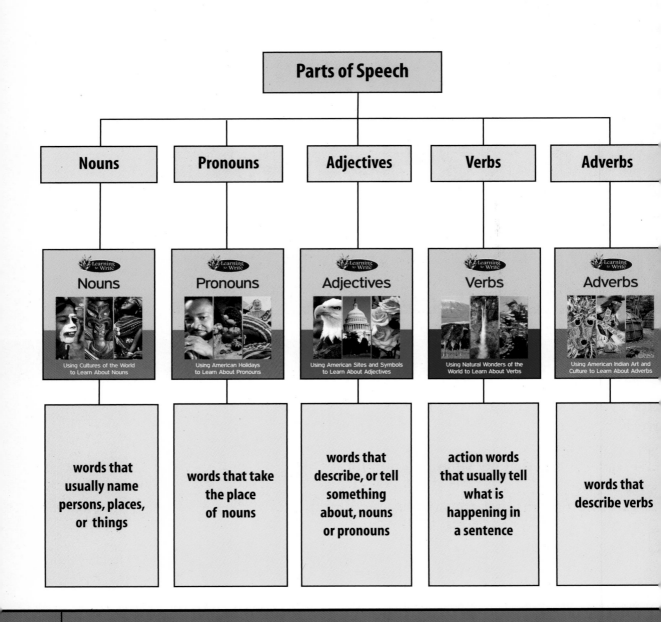

Parts of Speech

Nouns	**Pronouns**	**Adjectives**	**Verbs**	**Adverbs**
Nouns — Using Cultures of the World to Learn About Nouns	Pronouns — Using American Holidays to Learn About Pronouns	Adjectives — Using American Sites and Symbols to Learn About Adjectives	Verbs — Using Natural Wonders of the World to Learn About Verbs	Adverbs — Using American Indian Art and Culture to Learn About Adverbs
words that usually name persons, places, or things	words that take the place of nouns	words that describe, or tell something about, nouns or pronouns	action words that usually tell what is happening in a sentence	words that describe verbs

Further Research

Books

Many books provide information on nouns. To learn more about how to use different types of nouns, you can borrow books from the library. To learn more about indigenous people, try reading these books.

Braats, Rennay. *Maasai*. New York, NY: Weigl Publishers Inc., 2005.

Watson, Galadriel. *Mongols*. New York, NY: Weigl Publishers Inc., 2005.

Webster, Christine. *Polynesians*. New York, NY: Weigl Publishers Inc., 2004.

Websites

On the Internet, you can type terms, such as "nouns" or "types of nouns," into the search bar of your Web browser, and click the search button. It will take you to a number of sites with this information.

Read more about indigenous peoples at **http://cyberschoolbus.un.org/indigenous/index.asp** and **http://lanic.utexas.edu/region/indigenous**.

Glossary

ancestors: persons, plants, animals, or objects from a past generation

archery: the activity of shooting with bows and arrows

culture: a group of people who share customs, values, beliefs, and traditions

diet: the kind of foods that a person eats

environment: the area in which a person, animal, or plant exists or lives

fate: something that happens beyond a person's control

host: a person who receives or entertain other people as guests

hula: a dance performed by Hawai'ian women that includes six basic steps

indigenous peoples: the natives in a particular country or region

initiated: admitted into a society or group, often with special ceremonies

Index

Aboriginal Australians 5, 18, 19, 20

Inuit 7, 18, 20

Maasai 8, 14, 18, 21
Maori 6, 10, 18
Mongols 9, 11, 18

noun, person 4, 5, 6, 8, 9, 10, 11

noun, place 4, 5, 6, 8, 9, 10, 11
noun, thing 4, 5, 6, 8, 9, 10, 11
nouns, common 6, 10, 11, 15, 18, 21
nouns, plural 8, 9, 10, 11, 12, 14, 15, 21
nouns, possessive 6, 12, 13, 14, 15, 18, 21

nouns, proper 6, 8, 15, 18, 21
nouns, singular 8, 9, 10, 11, 12, 14, 15, 21

Polynesians 4, 15, 17, 18

Yanomami 12, 13, 16, 18, 19